Made in the USA
Las Vegas, NV
29 July 2021

27200514R00073